THIS BOOK
BELONGS TO:

_____

Silent Night

A Christmas Story

Written by L. E. McCullough Ph.D.
Illustrated by Cassandre Maxwell

Regina
Press

On a dark, rainy day in December, 1818, an old woman knelt in the Church of Saint Nicholas.

"...And, please, O Lord, allow the people in our village to be able to come tonight for Christmas Eve."

As she was finishing her prayers, Father Joseph Mohr came in, a psalm book under his arm. "Good morning, Frau Schmidt," he said pleasantly. "Will we see you tonight?"

"I hope I can come back this holy night, Father," she said, "But the weather has been bad with all this rain and melting snow."

"Yes it has been bad," agreed the priest, trying not to let his worry show. "We will miss you if you cannot come."

Frau Schmidt smiled, then blessed herself and went out into the driving rain.

All of a sudden, Herr Hummel, the church organist, burst in carrying one of the pipes. "Father Mohr! Father Mohr!" he cried.

"What is it, Herr Hummel? What's wrong?"

"Father, the organ is ruined! The dampness has rusted most of the pipes. And, the bellows have been nibbled by mice. The entire instrument is ruined. For Christmas Eve, there will be no organ."

The priest sighed deeply. "Without an organ there can be no choir."

"No choir, no music," moaned Herr Hummel.

"How can there not be music for Midnight Mass in the Church of Saint Nicholas?" lamented Father Mohr.

Just then, the church sexton, Herr Sirkir, rushed in.
His clothes were wet and muddy.

"I've been digging since daybreak, Father," he said.

"But with all this rain and melting snow, the river is

rising fast. I'm afraid the church could tear away from its foundation and collapse."

"What shall we do, Father?" asked the Sexton.

Father Mohr bowed his head a few moments.

"God knows we want to come together tonight and thank him for his precious gift of Jesus." he said.

"Right now, I don't have answers, but I know God will help us."

ot faraway, in his small cottage at the edge of the forest, Franz Gruber patiently instructed a young guitar student. "Very good, Anna." He said, "You are making beautiful music."

"I love the sound of the guitar," she said, stroking the instrument. "Why don't they allow it in church? They have organs and violins..."

"They say it is too common - a peasant instrument - not noble enough," sighed her teacher.

There was a loud knock at the door.

"To what do I owe this honor?" said Franz Gruber when he saw the priest. "I need you, my friend," said Father Mohr, shaking the rain off his cloak. "And I need your guitar."

As he explained the problem, Franz Gruber shook his head and chuckled in disbelief. "I am an untrained musician, Father. I play nothing but folk tunes."

"That may be true," said the priest, "but your folk music is beautiful and you are the only one I know who can help me write a song. We must have some music for

Soon the men began to toss thoughts back and forth to one another.

"The sky must have looked so bright when the angels appeared," said Franz Gruber.

"How quiet and calm it must have seemed in the stable," said Father Mohr.

"They say not even the animals made a sound," whispered Anna.

utside, the rain began to turn to snow as the temperature dropped, but no one in the cottage noticed.
Father Mohr, Franz Gruber and Anna were deep in thought picturing the light of the holy infant's face, the tenderness of Mary as she wrapped the Son of God in swaddling clothes and the glory of the angels as they spoke to the shepherds.

That night, everyone in the village made their way to the church for midnight mass. But, even though their feet crunched over new fallen snow, their hearts remained heavy, worried that the river would keeprising anyway.

It was hard to remember the words of the angel, "Do not be afraid, I bring you good news of great joy..."

"My friends," said Father Mohr, when they were all seated. "Tonight is different from the other Christmas Eves we have celebrated together. I know we are all a little afraid because of the weather and we are disappointed that our organ isn't working ... but, we can still make music and thank God for his gift to us."

"**H**ere is our humble offering," he continued. Then he nodded to Franz Gruber.

Softly, the two men joined their voices together.

> *"Silent night, holy night.*
> *All is calm, all is bright.*
> *Round yon Virgin,*
> *Mother and child.*
> *Holy Infant*
> *so tender and mild.*
> *Sleep in heavenly peace*
> *Sleep in heavenly peace."*

One by one, the congregation began to join in, their hearts touched by the simple words.

*S*uddenly, the church door flew open and Herr Sirkir burst in.

"The river! The river has gone down. It's a miracle!" The congregation sighed and exclaimed with relief.

"The town is saved!

Our church is saved!

God has heard our prayers."

Father Mohr raised his hands and eyes toward the ceiling. "Come my friends, let him hear our thanks! Everyone! Let's make this holy night ring with praise."

Silent night, holy night
Shepherds quake at the sight
Glories stream from heaven afar;
Heavenly hosts sing alleluia
Christ the Savior is born
Christ the Savior is born.

With tears of joy and happy smiles, the congregation of Saint Nicholas sang on never knowing their sweet new song would reach through the years to lighten hearts around the world, far faraway from the tiny village of Oberndorf.

Silent night, holy night.
All is calm, all is bright.
Round yon Virgin, Mother and child.
Holy Infant so tender and mild.
Sleep in heavenly peace
Sleep in heavenly peace."

Silent night, holy night
Shepherds quake at the sight
Glories stream from heaven afar;
Heavenly hosts sing alleluia
Christ the Savior is born
Christ the Savior is born.

Silent Night, holy night
Son of God, love's pure light.
Radiant beams from Thy holy face
With the dawn of redeeming grace.
Jesus, Lord, at Thy birth.
Jesus, Lord at Thy birth.

Silent night, holy night
All is calm, all is bright.
Round yon Virgin, Mother and Child;
Holy Infant so tender and mild.
Sleep in heavenly peace;
Sleep in heavenly peace.